2020 V

A Spiritual Awakening

By

Deborah Blanco

1. THE SHIFT
2. THE AWAKENING
3. THE CIRCLE
4. I DON'T NEED
5. NUMB
6. TREES
7. MEDIA
8. BRING BACK
9. SELF LOVE
10. PERFECTION
11. CAREFREE
12. SKYTRAILS
13. CHERISH
14. THE SYSTEM
15. AQUARIUS
16. GROUNDING
17. SLEEP
18. IN THE BEGINNING
19. LIFE
20. TALL TALES
21. WARRIORS
22. UNIVERSAL LAW
23. KUNDALINI
24. HUMANITY
25. ALL I CARE
26. SOUL SCHOOL
27. THINK
28. WORTHY
29. FOLLOW
30. FINAL DESTINATION

THE SHIFT

Brothers and sisters, it's time to shine,

The shift is here to make you align.

Connected as one we rise above,

To take back our world and fill it with love.

Our eyes are awakened we cannot unsee,

The ways of our world bequeath you and me.

Our mission to guide those that still sleep,

The prison of doubt and fear that they keep.

Love is our weapon, our mind is our sword,

Our strength is belief and faith in the Lord.

Together we stand, united we fight,

From out of the darkness, we follow the light.

THE AWAKENING

Awaken one morning to the earth's final shift,

I cannot explain, my words don't exist.

These feelings, emotions that run through my core,

My heart is so light my pain is no more.

The world they created is falling apart.

They tried to extract all the love from our heart.

Love and compassion our lessons to learn,

Empathic succession our journey to burn.

Run wild, run free our mind holds the key,

That unlock the chains that bind you and me.

The war is still raging, the evil is stalling,

The light of the angels has Lucifer falling,

His power diminished, his stealth is no more,

For Jesus our Saviour has opened the door.

THE CIRCLE

Our quest to fulfil this life, which is fake,

Subdued in our pool of misery we make.

Wake, eat, work, sleep,

A vicious circle we strive to keep.

Society has taken our freedom away,

It's time to wake up and fight for what may.

Light over dark, we take to the tower,

Which holds the true scripts of our history of power.

Our ancestors' plight, akashic realms to un-cover,

Can rejoice with the souls that connect to thy brother.

Seeds of the heavens like beacons of light

Have covered the earth with love pure and white.

I DON'T NEED

I don't need no fancy car,

Overpriced drinks in the flash new bar.

I don't need a highly paid job,

You work hard all week for the tax man to rob.

I don't need a pair of shoes cost a grand,

Or a bag, watch or t-shirt, advertising their brand.

I don't need no false fake friends,

No other way to spend their weekends.

I love the great outdoors,

Oceans, lakes, forests, moors.

My happiest moments surrounded by nature,

Given freely to us from God our creator.

NUMB

The earth is the source and origin of man,

Sun, moon and stars our story began.

Born in a world we need to suffice,

No memory, no purpose, no goal to devise.

Numbed down in slumber our vision impaired,

Our sub-conscious thoughts and words go unheard.

Complex the trauma which circles our mind,

Spinning like a cyclone unable to unwind.

Depression, Anxiety, P.T.S.D.

I don't understand why this happened to me.

Trapped in this cycle of negative thinking,

The doctors can't cure me so further I'm sinking.

I don't want no pills, potions or jabs,

Poisons manufactured man made in the labs.

Humanity's journey our lessons begin,

When you open your mind find your strength is within.

TREES

Trees are our life source, our connection, our fuel,

Grounded together, earths sacred jewel.

For she is alive with creatures all size,

From man, mammal, fish, insect, birds of the skies.

The purpose they say, for deforestation,

Cutting down trees to accommodate the population.

Giant Panda, Koala, no family, no home,

Nowhere to go nowhere to roam.

Nature's enigma is forest and sea,

It won't cost a penny the privilege is free.

The beauty surrounds, the earth will astound,

The pleasure of walking barefoot on the ground.

Sun, rain or hail, I will not fail,

To find my inner peace, on earth's holy grail.

MEDIA

Don't believe everything you hear on the news,

Media will control and manipulate your views.

Truth has been buried, censored, concealed,

To divide friend and family and create battlefield.

Don't believe everything you read in the paper,

Propaganda created to keep you from nature.

It's all doom and gloom to lower your mood,

And fuel your instinct to generate a feud.

Don't listen to gossip or spread what your told,

The universe hears you and gives you tenfold.

The world we reside can be beautiful and pure,

Let empathy, compassion and love be your cure.

BRING BACK

Bring back the summer of the seventies,

With skies of blue and days of long.

The laughter of the children,

That play in the streets and sing their song.

Bring back the music of the seventies,

Punk rock rebels and disco queens.

The fashion of the eighties,

Padded shoulders and Levi jeans.

Bring back the freedom of the seventies,

No mobile phones no Sky TV.

Bring back the simple way of life,

Bring it back and leave it be.

SELF LOVE

We need to learn to love ourselves,

The root of our connection.

What we emit comes back to us,

Like a mirror with our reflection.

We all have a purpose in life,

A reason to live, ability to love.

The most Powerful emotion of earth,

When love is given enough.

Always be kind, always be true,

Even to those that are awful to you.

These are the people that need it the most,

They are hurting inside, their pain is revealed,

We may be the key to unlock what's concealed.

PERFECTION

I look in the mirror, beauty I seek,

My reflection is ugly, my future is bleak.

I strive for perfection, my flaws are oblique,

My nose is obtrusive, not slender and sleek.

My teeth need improvement to fill in the gaps,

A trip to the dentist will cover them with caps.

My hair is receding, insecurity speeding,

My happiness fails me, false image conceding.

If only you knew, when your happy within,

Your journey of loving yourself will begin.

CAREFREE

I always believed in a life that was free,
Limitations, restrictions were not made for me.
I followed a path that was already mapped,
And set out on a journey I'd learn to adapt.

Childhood memories playing out on the street,
Kerby, British Bulldog, Tig, Hide and Seek.
Neighbours were friendly, loners were few,
Respect for our elders, the ones that we knew.

We helped one another, it didn't take long,
To shape a community dependable and strong.
Looking back now I can honestly say,
I'd hate to be part of youth culture today.

SKYTRAILS

The perfect precision,

Of jets on a mission.

The skies are awash,

With lines that cross.

Squares of blue,

We could see through.

But now the cloud,

Is all around.

Last all day,

The mist they spray.

Our sunny day,

Been sprayed away.

CHERISH

I cherish your body and clothe you so fine,

Jewellery of Diamonds straight from the mine.

Your home is a palace fit for a Queen,

The car that you drive is a pink limousine.

I cherish my family the love they provide,

The lessons I learn with them by my side.

My children, my world, will form my ancestry,

Friends come and go, my house never empty.

I ask for your time, of which I have none,

A life full of riches that too will be gone.

Take time alone, meditate, retreat,

The source of our being will need to replete.

Will you follow me to the afterlife?

Be with me till the end?

Yes, I'll be with you, I'll always be there,

Your soul, your trusted faithful friend.

THE SYSTEM

Certificate of birth, name and number,

You're in the system straight out of slumber.

Your put on a list in case u get sick,

And jabbed for diseases that no longer exist.

Enrolled in a school and taught to obey,

Your rota dictates when you work, eat and play.

Words in a textbook don't make any sense,

My memory serves me I'll pass through pretence.

No parents to greet you, no food in the fridge,

The Chinese left over's there's only a smidge.

You head to McDonald's you think it's a treat,

Their burgers are processed with carrion meat.

You build up your wall a prisoner within,

Uncertain, self-doubting, insecure in your skin.

Bound with a contract the straw man is victim,

This is our world you are slave to the system.

AQUARIUS

Aquarius, my star sign, unpredictable but true.

Deborah my name, busy bee in Hebrew.

My nature is random, my status is real,

I'm brutally honest but kind and surreal.

Off on a tangent, out on a whim,

I'll say I'm going shopping and head to the gym.

Plans are for builders, restrictions for site,

Dreams are for people with freedom of flight.

My life was a breeze is how I portray,

My struggles and strife I brush them away.

My parties were legend, my neighbours were deaf,

One side didn't hear me the others they left.

A positive mindset free spirit am I,

There's no holding me back I reach for the sky.

My happiest moments locked in my heart,

Is time spent with you until we do part.

GROUNDING

The earth is alive, it's energy within,

The core is a circuit we plug ourselves in.

Connected and grounded we return to the source,

And find that our mind has the power to enforce.

Barefoot on the ground or sit in meditation,

Natural healing to reduce inflammation.

Elements of the earth by way of infusion,

No longer a myth its scientifically proven.

Ten minutes a day on earth's natural lands,

Energy absorbs through our feet and our hands.

Our mind will find stillness, our health be improved,

Earths life force can heal you, when footwear removed.

SLEEP

Sleep is our Saviour,

Escape from the norm.

A world we control,

Our thoughts we conform.

We fall into slumber,

No longer a gender.

No money no status,

Just soul in its splendour.

We drift from reality,

Return to the source.

Our mind finds a stillness,

Our soul is on course.

IN THE BEGINNING

In the beginning,
In the blink of an eye.
The Universe existed,
An explosion in the sky.

Something came from nothing,
Separating day from night.
This could only happen if God said,
"Let there be light".

The heavens and the earth,
the oceans and the land.
A blueprint by design,
by God's divine own hand.

The creatures of the oceans,
the birds that fill the skies.
Vegetation, plants and trees,
the fuel to carbonize.

Humanity to rule,
Image of the lord.
The earth is now complete,
and fills what once was void.

LIFE

Life is precious, a god given gift,

And time is of the essence.

Gone way too fast quick as a flash,

From toddler to adolescent.

Don't worry what tomorrow brings,

Release your mind from matter.

Society demons slow you down,

Illusions made to shatter.

Your life will flash before your eyes,

One day will be your last.

Did I matter? was I loved?

Are questions you might ask.

When you look back through your life,

And you take your last breath.

Did u live your best life?

Are you ready for death?

19

TALL TALES

Two sides to every story,

Make sure you know the facts.

Gossip can be dangerous,

And have a grave impact.

A whisper can spread quickly,

Make sure you speak the truth.

Secrets are for keeping,

A friend will stay aloof.

The moral of this story,

To not speak bad at all.

If you can't be kind, be quiet,

Don't spread a tale so tall.

WARRIORS

Warriors of the galaxy,

Magnificent beings of light.

Incarnate on earth,

To fight for human right.

Born into a prison world,

No memory of your mission.

Black sheep, misfit, problem child,

You use your intuition.

Trauma is a trigger,

To free your troubled mind.

Society was your keeper,

Your here to help mankind.

Timing of the essence,

Bring forth the seeds of life.

To shine and raise vibration,

For earths ascension to contrive.

21

UNIVERSAL LAW

To understand universal law,

Think Energy, Frequency, Vibration.

To understand the way of the world,

Take evolution out of the equation.

A human computer network,

Advanced beyond our time.

The pineal gland antenna,

Will send and receive a sign.

Electromagnetic beings,

creation by design.

Thoughts and words we manifest,

Reality, we define.

KUNDALINI

An energetic pathway,

The Kundalini Line.

Connection centre chakras,

That travel through your spine.

Release your inner demons,

Free your troubled mind.

Breathwork and alignment,

Empower when combined.

Balance and find stillness,

Focus and explore.

Energy and vibration,

will penetrate your core.

Project your awareness,

Of spiritual realms.

A heavenly journey,

Exceeds and overwhelms.

HUMANITY

The scaremongering tactics of the media,

Devil's work in disguise.

The family unit is victim,

Television a series of lies.

The blackmail coercion of big pharma,

To jab every man woman and child.

An agenda of depopulation,

Has ceased now their plan has reviled.

Humanity is pulling together,

Battles subsiding, no longer fighting.

The loss of a loved one has family uniting,

The truth will prevail, the evil will fall,

For God, our Saviour,

Has answered our call.

ALL I CARE

I don't care If u don't brush your hair,

If u can't tell the time,

And your skin is fair.

I don't care if you can't organize,

If your clothes don't match,

Or the colour of your eyes.

I don't care for the high life you strive,

If you can't cook a meal,

Or the car that you drive.

All I care is the way that you greet,

If your friendly and true,

With the people you meet.

All I care is the time that you share,

If you spend it well,

With the people that care.

SOUL SCHOOL

Earth is a school,

We learn to evolve.

Born with no memory,

A puzzle to solve.

Connected as one,

Our souls will align.

The Universe hears you,

Just ask for a sign.

A positive mind,

A genuine heart.

The tools you need,

For lessons to start.

THINK

Do you think about life,

And how you were created.

Do you believe in God,

Or follow what's been stated.

Do you think about the past,

Ancient history, civilizations.

Or do you delve a little deeper,

Find discrepancy with calculations.

Do you think about the rich and famous,

Admire them from afar.

Do you see them as distraction,

Your happy who you are.

Do you think about your childhood,

And why you think this way.

Do you understand the path you chose,

Has woken you today.

WORTHY

Why hide your feelings, humanity's gift,

Sadness, depression to speak of will lift.

Why say your fine when you're hurting inside,

Your pain only deepens, your wounds open wide.

Why push away those around you that care,

True friends are like diamonds, their loyalty rare.

Why have you hidden behind that brick wall,

Your family and friends will be there if you fall.

Why let your mind control what you think,

You are the master the key to in sync.

Life on this earth, unique in its journey,

Is valued by God, he sees you are worthy.

FOLLOW

You sit in silence, you listen, you learn,

The message is clear with sense you discern.

You stand alone, your posture is strong,

Your mouth is engaged but you can't find your tongue.

You remove all emotion you can't get involved,

Your ego still haunts, you've not yet evolved.

You follow the crowd, fear has returned,

Whatever you say will be scorned and spurned.

FINAL DESTINATION

Be careful what you say or think,

Emission of vibration.

Can seal your fate with choice you make,

And receive your minds creation.

The human mind is multiverse,

A garden filled with choice.

Just waiting to be fertilized,

Activated by your voice.

The path you choose, no right or wrong,

Can be found through meditation.

Freewill choice in each dimension,

Will lead to the Final Destination.

Milton Keynes UK
Ingram Content Group UK Ltd.
UKHW020656290124
436892UK00018B/678